THE BOOK OF

COCKTAILS
VOLUME 2

THE BOOK OF

COCKTAILS

VOLUME 2

HILAIRE WALDEN

PHOTOGRAPHY BY

PATRICK McLEAVEY

HPBooks

ANOTHER BEST SELLING VOLUME FROM HPBOOKS

HPBooks
Published by the Berkley Publishing Group
A division of Penguin Putnam Inc.
375 Hudson Street
New York, NY 10014

Copyright © 2001 by Salamander Books Ltd.
By arrangement with Salamander Books Ltd.

A member of the Chrysalis Group plc

Project managed by: Stella Caldwell
Photographer: Patrick McLeavey
Designer: Sue Storey
Home Economist: Alex Winsor

First edition: October 2001

The Penguin Putnam Inc. World Wide Web site address is
http://www.penguinputnam.com

This book has been cataloged with the Library of Congress

ISBN 1-55788-372-6

Printed and bound in Spain

10 9 8 7 6 5 4 3 2 1

CONTENTS

FOREWORD

Cocktails have existed from at least the beginning of the 19th century. However, it was not until the Prohibition Era of the 1920s in the USA that cocktails, mixed alcoholic drinks, really began to take off, concocted to make palatable drinks from an assortment of poor quality liquors. The concept was soon seized upon by people who had access to good quality liquor. Then, with the lifting of the alcochol ban in 1933 and the raising of overall standards of liquor, many of the more acceptable recipes were refined, and more were created. The cocktail boom was soon imitated around the world.

Cocktails have an enduring appeal. Although they faded slightly from fashion in the '50s and '60s their popularity returned in the mid to late '70s, and today they are ideal for contemporary lifestyles.

People are entertaining at home more than ever, and occasions are often kept casual: a few friends drop in for supper rather than dress up for dinner, or people might just call in for a drink before lunch or in the evening. Now that wine-drinking is taken for granted, serving a cocktail is an ideal way of giving guests something that is a little different and special, both at relaxed and at more formal occasions. Those who eschew a traditional spirit as a digestive, may well enjoy rounding off a meal with a cocktail. If you only have one guest and don't want to open up a fresh bottle of wine, or have no suitably chilled wine in reserve, then a cocktail can be the perfect solution.

Cocktails are fun: it is not always necessary to have an extensive range of drinks to hand, and making them is easier than you might imagine. The book explains how to substitute everyday items for specialist cocktail-making and measuring equipment, and shows that cocktail recipes are not sacrosanct, but can be modifed to suit personal tastes and adapted using ingredients that are available.

The Book of Cocktails, Volume 2 contains recipes both for classic cocktails such as Manhattan and Old-fashioned, and for more recent creations. Some cocktails require just a couple of ingredients while others are more complicated. There is also a selection of non-alcoholic drinks.

—— INTRODUCTION ——

EQUIPMENT

Measure: The volume of a standard bar measure varies between countries but is usually about 3 tablespoons. However it does not matter what size of measure you use providing it remains consistent throughout the making of a drink. A jigger is ideal. When making the same type of cocktail for several people, it is more practical to use a measuring cup from the kitchen for large amounts, such as fruit juice.

Cocktail shaker: Usually made of stainless steel, this consists of two parts that fit together, with an integral strainer. To use, add the ice and stipulated ingredients, hold the two parts together with both hands and shake briskly until the shaker becomes frosted on the outside. Strain immediately into a glass. A screw-top jar can be improvised.

Screw-top jar: Choose one that has a neck that is wide enough for ice to be added with ease.

Strainer: A bartender's strainer is made of stainless steel. It has a springy wire edge and the surface with the holes is flat, not curved. A small nylon or stainless steel sieve can be substituted.

Other useful equipment: The following items will be useful: mixing glass, long-handled spoon for stirring drinks, cocktail sticks for decorations, drinking straws, teaspoon, tablespoon, stainless steel vegetable knife, small chopping board for cutting lemons etc., fruit juice squeezer, heatproof glass to hold hot water in which to rinse spoons used for mixing drinks, tea towel, dish cloth, paper towels, corkscrew, bottle opener, closure for sparkling wines, ice bucket or similar insulated container, drip mats.

INGREDIENTS

When a particular brand is specified, for example of an orange liqueur, other brands may be substituted.

Choose drinks that you will use most frequently, especially liqueurs. To keep costs down, buy half or quarter bottles where possible. Miniatures of some liqueurs are available, but they are expensive.

Most useful alcoholic drinks: Gin; vodka; rum (both dark and white); brandy; whisky; dry vermouth; sweet vermouth; crème de menthe; at least one orange liqueur such as Curacao, Cointreau, or Grand Marnier; Amaretto di Seranno; cherry brandy; apricot brandy; crème de cacao; Tia Maria or Kahlua; and Galliano.

Mixers: Soda water, lemonade, tonic

water, ginger ale and grenadine.
Extras: Angostura bitters and orange bitters.

GLASSES

There are a great many styles and shapes of glasses and although there are some classic combinations of glasses and cocktails, such as Dry Martini in a cocktail glass, or an Old-fashioned in an old-fashioned glass, in general the style and shape of glass that is used is not all that important. However, the glass should be spotlessly clean, and free from any detergent or odor. When glasses are stored upside down, air that is trapped in the bowl can become stale and affect the smell and taste of a drink that is later made in them. If glasses have been stored upside down for any length of time, rinse them before use.

Colored glasses and those that are heavily patterned, can detract from the appearance, and therefore part of the enjoyment, of a drink. It is also a good idea to choose a glass that will be no more than two-thirds full when both the ice and the drink have been added. On the other hand, do not use a very tall glass or a chunky goblet for a small volume of a delicate cocktail.

TYPES OF GLASSES THAT ARE TRADITIONALLY USED :
Cocktail glass: Classically the bowl of these stemmed glasses is 'V'-shaped, but it can be any shape if it has a capacity of about ½ cup.
Old-fashioned: Traditionally this tumbler has sloping sides and holds about ¾-1 cup.
Whisky tumbler: Similar to an old-fashioned glass but with straight sides.
Highball: This is a tall, straight-sided tumbler holding about 1½ cups.
Champagne flute: The shape of bowl that finds favor today is tall and slim and curves slightly towards the rim. This is preferable to the old-fashioned saucer-shaped bowl, where the Champagne bubbles would disappear rapidly, and the drink would warm too quickly.
Wine glass or 'tulip' glass: A number of different sizes are available, but an average size has a capacity of between ½-¾ cup.
Liqueur glass: This can be useful as a measure but is not used for cocktails.
Brandy balloon: Brandy balloons are available in a range of sizes. Their inward curving bowls are designed to trap in the vapor and aroma of a drink.

MAKING COCKTAILS

Cocktail-making is not difficult, but your task will be easier, and more successful if a few basic steps are observed:
• Keep all drinks in a cool place; if

possible, mixers should be kept in the refrigerator.

• Use chilled glasses. To chill glasses quickly, fill them with cracked ice for a few minutes. Tip away the ice and dry the glasses thoroughly before using.

• A 'dash' is the amount released in a quick squirt from a bottle.

• Prepare drinks on a surface that will not be spoilt if marked by bottles, glasses or drips, and can be wiped easily.

• Always add ice to a cocktail shaker or screw-top jar.

• The more ice that is used the cooler the drink will be, but too much ice, especially if crushed, will dilute the drink.

• Crushed ice cools a drink more, and more quickly, than cracked ice.

• With very few exceptions, always strain cocktails that have been shaken, to remove the ice, fragments of fruit flesh and other particles.

• Use clean ice.

• Ordinary water sometimes makes cloudy ice cubes. If this happens, use mineral water.

• Avoid using the same ice in a shaker for different types of drinks, because any liquid adhering to the surface of the ice will taint the next drink.

• Generally, clear drinks are stirred, while those containing ingredients that will make the drink cloudy, such as fruit juices, egg white and cream are shaken or mixed in a blender.

• Wash shakers, or mixing glasses and stirrers between preparing different types of drinks.

• Keep a container of warm water handy for rinsing spoons etc.

• If planning to decorate a drink elaborately and serve it with straws, as may be the case for an 'exotic' recipe, choose a substantial tumbler or goblet rather than a delicate glass or one with a narrow neck.

• Avoid filling glasses to the brim. This obviously makes drinking difficult and the drink may be spilt.

• When serving drinks that contain a lot of ice, or if the rim of the glass is frosted, add drinking straws to the glass.

• Taste is subjective, so if you are not particularly keen on a cocktail, rather than abandon it, alter the proportions of ingredients in the drink. Alternatively substitute other ingredients to make the cocktail more to your taste.

SPECIAL PREPARATIONS

Cracked ice: Put the required number of ice cubes in a strong plastic bag and close the end of the bag. Bring the bag down sharply on a firm surface, or hit it with a heavy implement. Alternatively, use a food processor.

Crushed ice: This is prepared in the same way as cracked ice, but is broken more finely. A blender can also be used.

Powdered sugar: Briefly grind granulated sugar in a blender or food processor. Powdered sugar is useful in that it dissolves more quickly and readily than ordinary sugar in drinks that are not stirred, or only stirred briefly.

Simple sugar syrup: Dissolve powdered sugar in an equal amount of warm water.

FROSTING GLASSES

Ensure that the glass is always held upside down by the stem to prevent the juice running down the bowl of the glass.

Salt: wipe around the outside of the rim with a lemon or lime wedge. Put a layer of salt in a saucer and dip the glass rim in the salt until evenly coated.

Sugar: For a sweeter frosting, wipe the rim of the glass with a lemon or lime wedge, or alternatively dip the rim into lightly beaten egg white. Grenadine may also be used. Put a layer of superfine sugar on a saucer, then dip the glass rim in the sugar until evenly coated. For extra effect, the sugar can be colored with edible food coloring.

Coffee: Dip the rim of the glass in lightly beaten egg white, then into powder instant coffee or finely ground coffee beans, or cocoa powder. Do not use granular coffee.

Coconut: Dip the rim of the glass into lightly beaten egg white, then immediately into a saucer of unsweetened shredded coconut. If desired, the coconut can be lighty toasted or alternatively colored with edible food coloring.

Warning: It is possible that raw eggs may contain salmonella. They should never be served to anyone with a serious illness or compromised immune system.

lemon juice

sugar

lemon juice and sugar

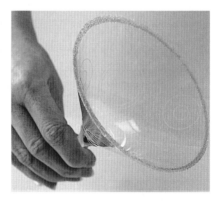

grenadine and sugar

DECORATION

The appearance of a drink is very important. With a few, such as 'Old-fashioned', the decoration is an integral part of the recipe, but in the majority of cases it can be varied according to what is available. However, try to keep it appropriate to the type and flavor of the cocktail.

Avoid using canned fruits, because unless the fruit has been dried on paper towels extremely well, the syrup from them is liable to drip into the cocktail and the sweetness will upset the balance of flavors. Many people eat the decoration in between sips of a drink, and this will also detract from the intended taste of the cocktail.

Decorative ice cubes: Any decoration should complement the drink(s) being made. Suitable decorations can be shapes cut from orange, lemon or lime peels, mint leaves and small pieces of fresh fruit.

Half-fill an ice cube tray with water, and freeze. Dip the chosen decoration (which should complement the drink) in water, place on the ice cube and return to the freezer until frozen. Fill the tray with water and freeze.

── HARVEY WALLBANGER ──

cracked ice
fresh orange juice
1 measure vodka
½ measure Galliano

Fill a tall glass with cracked ice. Pour orange juice over ice until glass is three-quarters full.

Add vodka to glass and stir. Pour Galliano on top of drink so that it floats; do not stir.

Serves 1

─── BEHIND THE WALL ───

4 ice cubes, cracked
1 measure fresh orange juice
1 measure vodka
½ measure Mandarin Napoleon liqueur
½ measure Galliano
ginger ale, for topping up

Put ice into a cocktail shaker or screw-top jar. Pour orange juice, vodka, Mandarin Napoleon and Galliano into shaker or jar. Shake together to mix.

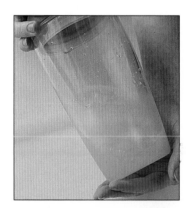

Strain cocktail into a glass and top up with ginger ale.

Serves 1

—— RUSSIAN SECRET ——

4 ice cubes, cracked
½ measure vodka
½ measure Benedictine
2 measures unsweetened fresh grapefruit juice

Put half the ice cubes into a cocktail shaker or screw-top jar. Pour vodka and Benedictine into shaker or jar. Add grapefruit juice. Shake to mix ingredients.

Put remaining ice into a small tumbler. Strain in cocktail. Serve with a short straw.

Serves 1

CZARINE

3 ice cubes, cracked
1 measure vodka
½ measure apricot brandy
½ measure dry vermouth
dash orange bitters
TO DECORATE:
orange slice
apricot slice

Put ice cubes into a cocktail shaker or
screw-top jar. Pour vodka, apricot brandy
and vermouth into shaker or jar. Add
bitters. Shake to mix.

Strain drink into a glass. Decorate with
orange and apricot slices.

Serves 1

BLUE LAGOON

4 ice cubes
1 measure vodka
1 measure blue curaçao
lemonade, for topping up

Put ice cubes into a small goblet. Pour vodka and blue curaçao over ice cubes. Stir to mix.

Top up drink with lemonade.

Serves 1

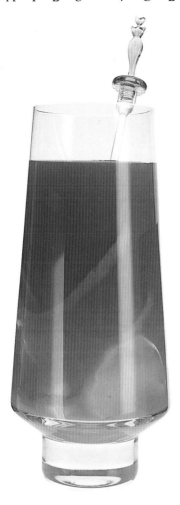

SLOE DANCE

1 measure vodka
½ measure Southern Comfort
½ measure sloe gin
fresh orange juice, for topping up
spirals of orange rind, to decorate
3 ice cubes, cracked

Pour vodka, Southern Comfort and sloe gin
into a mixing glass. Stir ingredients to mix.

Put ice cubes into a tall glass. Pour drink
into glass. Top up with fresh orange juice.
Stir. Decorate with spirals of orange peel.

Serves 1

CRANBERRY COOLER

1 measure vodka
2 measures cranberry juice
juice of 1 lime
2 ice cubes, cracked

Pour vodka, cranberry juice and lime juice into a mixing glass. Stir ingredients to mix.

Put ice cubes into a glass. Pour drink into glass. Stir.

Serves 1

GREEN ANGEL

¾ measure vodka
⅓ measure dry vermouth
⅓ measure crème de menthe

Put ice into a mixing glass. Pour vodka, vermouth and crème de menthe into mixing glass. Stir ingredients to mix.

Strain drink into a cocktail glass.

Serves 1

MARK ONE

2 ice cubes, cracked
½ measure vodka
½ measure Green Chartreuse
½ measure Cinzano Bianco
1 ice cube, cracked

Put ice into a mixing glass. Pour vodka, Green Chartreuse and Cinzano into mixing glass.

Stir ingredients to mix. Strain drink into a cocktail glass.

Serves 1

VODKATINI

3 ice cubes, cracked
2 measures vodka
¼-½ measure dry vermouth
1 lemon slice, twisted

Put ice into a cocktail shaker or screw top jar. Pour vodka and martini into shaker or jar. Shake to mix ingredients.

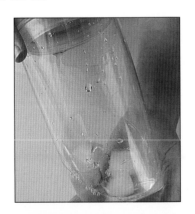

Strain cocktail into a cocktail glass. Decorate rim of glass with lemon.

Serves 1

——— WHITE RUSSIAN ———

5 ice cubes, cracked
1 measure vodka
1 measure Tia Maria
1 measure milk or heavy cream
3 chocolate dragees
drinking straws, to serve

Put half the ice into a cocktail shaker or screw-top jar. Pour vodka and Tia Maria into shaker or jar. Add milk or cream. Shake to mix ingredients.

Put remaining ice into a tall, slim glass. Strain cocktail into glass. Float dragees on drink and serve with straws.

Serves 1

— BLACK RUSSIAN —

cracked ice
2 measures vodka
1 measure crème de cacao, such as Tia Maria or
  Kahlua

Put some cracked ice into a glass.

Pour vodka and crème de cacao over ice.
Stir to mix.

Serves 1

─── NORMAN CONQUEROR ───

4 ice cubes, cracked
1 measure vodka
½ measure calvados
½ measure unsweetened apple juice
dash Angostura bitters
TO DECORATE:
apple slice
lemon slice

Put ice cubes into a cocktail or screw-top jar. Pour vodka and calvados into shaker or jar. Add apple juice and bitters. Shake to mix.

Put remaining ice into a tall glass. Strain cocktail into glass. Decorate with apple and lemon slices.

Serves 1

AUTUMN

4 ice cubes, cracked
1¼ measures vodka
¾ measure Southern Comfort
2 teaspoons fresh lemon juice
twist of lemon rind, to decorate

Put half the ice into a cocktail shaker or
screw-top jar. Pour vodka and Southern
Comfort into shaker or jar. Add lemon
juice. Shake to mix ingredients.

Put remaining ice into a cocktail glass.
Strain cocktail into glass. Decorate rim of
glass with lemon peel.

Serves 1

GODMOTHER

2 ice cubes
1 measure vodka
1 measure Amaretto di Saronno

Put ice cubes into a small tumbler.

Pour vodka and Amaretto over ice. Stir cocktail to mix.

Serves 1

PIONEER

3 ice cubes
½ measure vodka
½ measure Drambuie
½ measure curaçao

Put ice cubes into a cocktail shaker or screw-top jar. Pour vodka, Drambuie and curaçao into shaker or jar.

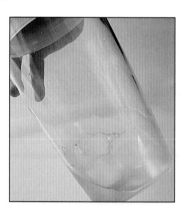

Shake drink to mix. Strain drink into a glass.

Serves 1

DRY MARTINI

cracked ice
2 measures gin
½ measure dry vermouth
TO DECORATE:
strip of lemon rind
1 green olive

Put cracked ice into a mixing glass. Pour gin and vermouth over. Stir.

Strain drink into a cocktail glass. Hang strip of lemon rind over rim of glass so one end is in cocktail, or place it in glass. Add olive.

Variation: For a Sweet Martini, shake a few drops of orange bitters into a cocktail glass and swirl around to coat sides of glass. Add 2 measures gin and 1 measure sweet vermouth. Stir to mix. Decorate with a cocktail cherry.

Serves 1

FALLEN ANGEL

3 ice cubes, cracked
1½ measures gin
½ measure lemon juice
4 dashes crème de menthe

Put ice cubes into a cocktail shaker or screw-top jar. Pour gin, lemon juice and crème de menthe into shaker or jar. Shake to mix.

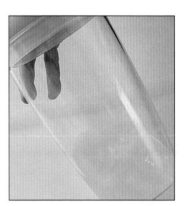

Strain drink into a cocktail glass.

Serves 1

BULLDOG

3 ice cubes, cracked
½ measure gin
1 measure cherry brandy
juice ½ lemon

Put ice cubes into a cocktail shaker or screw-top jar. Pour gin and cherry brandy into shaker or jar. Shake to mix.

Strain drink into a cocktail glass.

Serves 1

———— BLACK GYPSY ————

2 ice cubes, cracked
⅔ measure gin
⅓ measure Mandarin Napoleon liqueur
⅓ measure fresh lemon juice
5 drops Ricard or other pastis

Put ice cubes into a cocktail shaker or screw-top jar. Pour gin and Mandarin Napoleon into shaker or jar. Add lemon juice and Ricard. Shake to mix.

Strain drink into a glass.

Serves 1

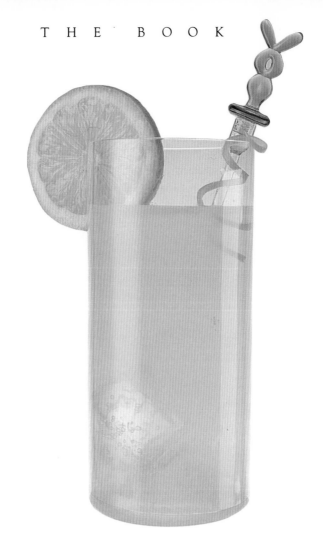

GIN SLING

juice of ½ lemon
1 measure gin
2 teaspoons powdered sugar (see page 10)
dash Angostura bitters (optional)
1 ice cube
mineral water or soda water

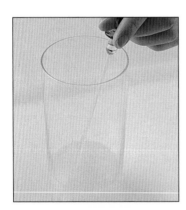

Put lemon juice, sugar and gin in a tall tumbler. Stir ingredients to dissolve sugar. Add bitters, if liked.

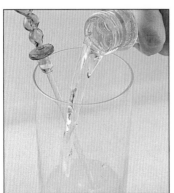

Add ice cube and top up with mineral water or soda water.

Serves 1

STRAWBERRY DAWN

crushed ice
1 measure gin
1 measure coconut cream
3 large, ripe strawberries
lime or lemon juice, to taste
strawberry, to decorate

Put ice, gin, coconut cream and strawberries into a blender. Mix together.

Add lemon or lime juice, to taste. Pour into a cocktail glass. Decorate with a strawberry. Serve with straws.

Serves 1

CITRUS GIN SLING

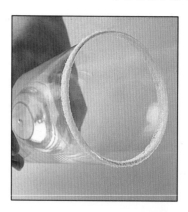

⅔ cup fresh lemon juice
⅔ cup fresh lime juice
⅔ cup gin
2 tablespoons superfine sugar
soda water or mineral water, for topping up
TO SERVE:
ice cubes
6 glasses, rims frosted (see page 10)
TO DECORATE:
lemon slices
lime slices

Put some ice into a cocktail shaker or screw-top jar.

Pour lemon juice, lime juice and gin into shaker or jar. Add superfine sugar. Shake well. Put ice cubes into frosted tall glasses (see page 10). Strain over gin mixture. Top up with soda water or mineral water. Decorate glasses with lemon and lime slices.

Serves 6

WHITE LADY

2 ice cubes, cracked
1 measure gin
½ measure Cointreau
juice of ½ lemon
dash of egg white (see page 11)

Put ice cubes into a cocktail shaker or screw-top jar. Pour gin and Cointreau into shaker or jar. Add egg white. Shake to mix.

Strain drink into a cocktail glass.

Serves 1

WATERMELON SLING

¼ watermelon
5 ice cubes, crushed
¼ cup gin
1 tablespoon superfine sugar
juice ½ lime

Discard seeds from watermelon. Scoop flesh into a blender.

Add ice, gin, sugar and lime juice. Blend until smooth. Pour drink into 2 chilled glasses.

Serves 2

ETON BLAZER

3 ice cubes, cracked
1¼ measures gin
⅓ measure kirsch
2 tablespoons lemon juice
1-2 teaspoons powdered sugar (see page 10)
soda water, for topping up
2 ice cubes, to serve

Put cracked ice into a cocktail shaker or screw-top jar. Pour gin and kirsch into shaker or jar. Add lemon juice and sugar and shake to mix ingredients.

Put ice cubes into a tumbler. Strain cocktail into tumbler and top up with soda water.

Serves 1

ORANGE BLOSSOM

3 ice cubes, cracked
1 measure gin
1 measure bianco vermouth
1 measure fresh orange juice
1-2 ice cubes
1 orange slice, to decorate

Put quarter of ice into a cocktail shaker or screw-top jar. Pour gin and vermouth into shaker or jar. Add orange juice. Shake to mix.

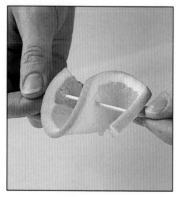

Put remaining ice into a tall, narrow tumbler. Strain cocktail into tumbler. Twist orange slice and decorate rim of glass.

Serves 1

—— SNAKE IN THE GRASS ——

3 ice cubes, cracked
½ measure gin
½ measure Cointreau
½ measure dry vermouth
½ measure lemon juice

Put ice cubes into a cocktail shaker or screw-top jar. Pour gin, Cointreau, dry vermouth and lemon juice into shaker or jar. Shake to mix.

Strain drink into a cocktail glass.

Serves 1

RED KISS

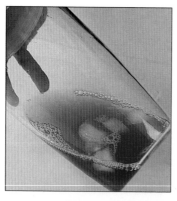

3 ice cubes, cracked
½ measure gin
½ measure cherry brandy
1 measure dry vermouth, preferably Noilly Prat
TO DECORATE:
twist of lemon peel
fresh cherry or maraschino cherry

Put ice into a cocktail shaker or screw-top jar. Pour gin, cherry brandy and vermouth into shaker or jar. Shake to mix.

Strain drink into cocktail glass. Decorate drink with a strip of lemon rind and a fresh cherry or a maraschino cherry.

Serves 1

THE VISITOR

3 ice cubes
½ measure gin
½ measure Cointreau
½ measure crème de banane
1 dash fresh orange juice
1 egg white (see page 11)
TO DECORATE:
banana slices
twisted orange slices

Put ice cubes into a cocktail shaker or screw-top jar. Pour gin, Cointreau and crème de banane into shaker or jar and add orange juice and egg white. Shake to mix.

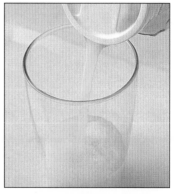

Strain drink into a glass. Decorate with banana slices and twisted orange slices.

Serves 1

BARBERA

5 ice cubes, cracked
1 measure bourbon whiskey
¾ measure Drambuie
½ measure Amaretto di Saronno
2 dashes orange bitters
strip of lemon rind
1 orange slice, to decorate

Put half the ice into a cocktail shaker or
screw-top jar. Pour whiskey, Drambuie, and
Amaretto into shaker or screw-top jar. Add
bitters. Shake to mix.

Put remaining ice into a tumbler. Strain
drink into glass. Squeeze zest from orange
rind onto surface of drink. Decorate with
orange slice.

Serves 1

MINT JULEP

3 sprigs mint
½ teaspoon superfine sugar
1 tablespoon soda water
2-3 ice cubes, crushed
1 measure bourbon whiskey
mint sprig, to decorate

In a glass, crush mint with sugar until sugar has dissolved, then rub around inside of glass. Discard mint.

Stir soda water into sugar to dissolve sugar. Put ice into glass. Pour bourbon over ice; do not stir. Decorate with mint sprig.

Serves 1

GODFATHER

2 ice cubes
1 measure Scotch whisky
1 measure Amaretto di Saronno

Put ice into a tumbler.

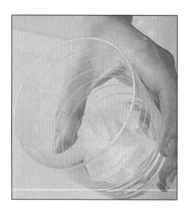

Pour whisky and amaretto over ice. Stir to mix.

Serves 1

OLD FASHIONED

1 sugar lump
1-2 drops Angostura bitters
1-2 ice cubes
1 measure Scotch whisky
½ slice orange

Put sugar cube into a tumbler. Shake bitters over sugar and stir until sugar has dissolved.

Add ice cubes to tumbler and stir to coat with liquid. Add whisky. Stir lightly then float orange slice on top.

Serves 1

MANHATTAN

cracked ice
2 measures rye whisky
1 measure sweet vermouth
dash Angostura bitters
TO DECORATE:
1 maraschino cherry
strip of lemon rind

Put some cracked ice into a glass. In a mixing glass or a tumbler, mix together whisky, vermouth and bitters. Pour over ice.

Stir cocktail once. Put maraschino cherry and lemon rind on to a cocktail stick and add to drink.

Serves 1

Variation: To make a dry version, use dry vermouth.

RUSTY NAIL

2-3 ice cubes
1 measure Scotch whisky
½ measure Drambuie
twist of lemon rind, to decorate

Put ice into a small tumbler. Pour whisky over ice. Pour Drambuie over the back of a teaspoon on to the top of whisky.

Decorate rim of glass with a twist of lemon rind.

Serves 1

CAPRICORN

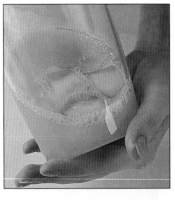

4 ice cubes, cracked
1 measure bourbon whiskey
½ measure apricot brandy
2 measures fresh orange juice
½ measure fresh lemon juice
1 orange slice, to decorate

Put 2 ice cubes into a cocktail shaker or screw-top jar. Pour whiskey and apricot brandy into shaker or jar. Add orange juice and lemon juice. Shake to mix ingredients.

Put remaining ice into an old-fashioned glass. Strain cocktail into glass. Decorate with orange slice.

Serves 1

PEACH FIZZ

2-3 ice cubes, cracked
1 measure brandy
½ measure peach brandy
½ measure kirsch
2 measures fresh orange juice
soda water, for topping up
TO DECORATE:
peach slices
orange slices
maraschino cherries

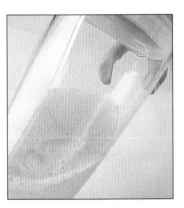

Put ice into a cocktail shaker or screw-top jar. Pour brandy, peach brandy, kirsch and orange juice into a shaker or jar. Shake.

Strain cocktail into a tall glass. Top up with soda water. Decorate with peach slices, orange slices and maraschino cherries.

Serves 1

BRANDY ALEXANDER

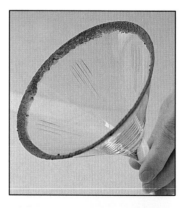

3 ice cubes, cracked
½ measure cream
½ measure brandy
½ measure crème de cacao or Tia Maria
1 chocolate stick, to serve
TO DECORATE:
beaten egg white
finely grated or chopped plain chocolate or cocoa
    powder mixed with superfine sugar, or ground
    coffee beans

Frost a cocktail glass with grated or chopped chocolate or cocoa mixed with superfine sugar, or coffee (see page 11).

Put cracked ice into a cocktail shaker or screw-top jar. Pour the cream, brandy and crème de cacao into shaker or jar. Shake to mix. Strain drink into glass. Add the chocolate stick.

Serves 1

VIKING

2-3 ice cubes, cracked
¾ measure brandy
¾ measure Benedictine
¾ measure dry vermouth, preferably Noilly Prat
wide strip of lemon rind
fine strips of lemon rind, to decorate

Put ice cubes into a mixing glass. Pour in brandy, Benedictine and vermouth. Stir ingredients and ice together. Strain into a cocktail glass.

Squeeze wide strip of lemon rind on to drink. Decorate with fine strips of lemon rind.

Serves 1

BRANDY FIX

1 teaspoon confectioners' sugar
1 teaspoon water
1 measure brandy
½ measure cherry brandy
juice of ½ lemon
ice cubes
1 slice lemon, to decorate

Dissolve sugar in the water in a mixing glass or tumbler. Add brandy, cherry brandy and lemon juice. Stir to mix ingredients.

Fill a glass with ice cubes. Strain in cocktail. Float lemon slice on top and add a straw.

Serves 1

BETWEEN THE SHEETS

2-3 ice cubes, cracked
½ measure brandy
½ measure white rum
½ measure Cointreau
1 tablespoon fresh orange juice

Put ice into a cocktail shaker or screw-top jar. Pour brandy, white rum and Cointreau into shaker or jar. Add orange juice. Shake to mix.

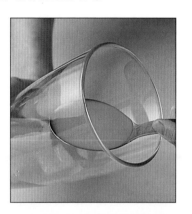

Strain cocktail into a cocktail glass.

Serves 1

LEO

2-3 ice cubes, crushed
1 measure brandy
½ measure Amaretto di Saronno
1½ measures fresh orange juice
soda water, for topping up

Put ice into a cocktail shaker or screw-top
jar. Pour brandy and Amaretto into shaker
or jar. Add orange juice. Shake drink to
mix.

Strain into a glass. Top up with soda water.
Pour Campari on top of drink; do not stir.

Serves 1

HONEYMOON

2-3 ice cubes, cracked
1 measure calvados
½ measure Benedictine
1 teaspoon Cointreau
2 teaspoons fresh orange juice

Put ice cubes into a cocktail shaker or screw-top jar. Pour calvados, Benedictine and Cointreau into shaker or jar. Add orange juice. Shake to mix.

Strain drink into a glass.

Serves 1

SHANGHAI

3 ice cubes, crushed
1 measure brandy
½ measure curaçao
¼ measure maraschino
2 dashes Angostura bitters
TO DECORATE:
piece of lemon rind
1 maraschino cherry

Put ice cubes in a cocktail shaker or screw-top jar. Pour in brandy, curaçao and maraschino. Add Angostura bitters. Shake to mix ingredients.

Strain drink into a cocktail glass. Decorate with lemon peel and maraschino cherry.

Serves 1

CORPSE REVIVER

2-3 ice cubes
1 measure brandy
½ measure Calvados
½ measure sweet vermouth

Put ice cubes into a cocktail shaker or screw-top jar. Pour brandy, Calvados and sweet vermouth into shaker or jar. Shake to mix.

Strain drink into a cocktail glass.

Serves 1

SIDECAR

3 ice cubes, cracked
1 measure brandy
½ measure Cointreau
½ measure lemon juice

Put cracked ice cubes into a cocktail shaker or screw-top jar. Pour brandy, Cointreau and lemon juice into shaker or jar. Shake to mix.

Strain drink into a cocktail glass.

Serves 1

TEMPTATION

2-3 ice cubes, cracked
½ measure brandy
1 measure Grand Marnier
1 teaspoon lemon juice
TO DECORATE:
beaten egg white
superfine sugar
½ orange slice
½ lemon slice

Frost rim of glass (see page 11). Put ice cubes into a cocktail shaker or screw-top jar. Pour brandy and Grand Marnier into shaker or jar. Add lemon juice. Shake to mix.

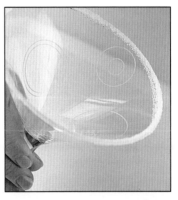

Strain drink into a glass. Decorate with ½ orange slice and ½ lemon slice. Serve with a short straw.

Serves 1

KCB

2 ice cubes, cracked
1 measure brandy
⅓ measure kirsch
2 dashes apricot brandy
½ lemon

Put ice cubes into a mixing glass. Pour brandy and kirsch over ice. Add apricot brandy and stir to mix.

Strain drink into a glass. Squeeze a little lemon juice on top.

Serves 1

APPLE SHOWER

2-3 ice cubes
1 measure brandy
1 measure Benedictine
2 measures unsweetened apple juice
soda water, for topping up

Put ice into a cocktail shaker or screw-top jar. Pour brandy and Benedictine into shaker or jar. Add apple juice. Shake to mix.

Strain drink into a glass. Top up with soda water.

Serves 1

CALVADOS SMASH

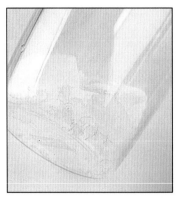

2-3 ice cubes, cracked
1 measure calvados
2 measures unsweetened apple juice
1 teaspoon lemon juice
1 teaspoon sugar syrup (see page 10)
1 dash orange bitters

Put ice into a cocktail shaker or screw-top jar. Pour calvados, apple juice, lemon juice and sugar syrup into shaker or jar. Add bitters. Shake to mix.

Strain drink into a glass.

Serves 1

STINGER

3 ice cubes, cracked
¾ measure brandy
¼ measure white crème de menthe

Put cracked ice cubes into a cocktail shaker or screw-top jar. Pour brandy and white crème de menthe into shaker or jar. Shake to mix.

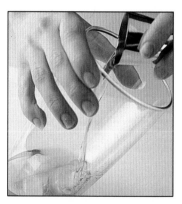

Strain drink into a cocktail glass.

Serves 1

GENOESE ADMIRAL

3 ice cubes, cracked
1½ measures dark rum
½ measure sweet vermouth
2 teaspoons fresh orange juice
1 teaspoon fresh lemon juice
TO DECORATE:
thin strip of orange rind
thin strips of lemon rind

Put ice cubes in a cocktail shaker or screw-top jar. Pour rum and sweet vermouth into shaker or jar. Add orange juice and lemon juice. Shake to mix ingredients.

Strain drink into a cocktail glass. Decorate glass with orange and lemon rinds.

Serves 1

BLUE HAWAIIAN

crushed ice
1 measure white rum
1 measure blue curaçao
2 measures pineapple juice
1 measure coconut cream
TO DECORATE:
strip of coconut
piece of pineapple

Put ice into a cocktail shaker or screw-top
jar. Pour white rum, curaçao, pineapple
juice and coconut cream into shaker or jar.
Shake to mix.

Strain cocktail into a glass.

Serves 1

MR GIOVANI

½ measure dark rum
½ measure sweet vermouth
¼ measure dry vermouth
1 tablespoon fresh orange juice
1 teaspoon lime cordial

Put cracked ice cubes into a cocktail shaker or screw-top jar. Pour rum and vermouths into shaker or jar. Add orange juice and lime cordial. Shake to mix.

Strain cocktail into a glass.

Serves 1

— MORROS —

fresh lime juice
powdered sugar (see page 10)
3 ice cubes, cracked
1 measure dark rum
½ measure gin
1 measure pineapple juice
TO DECORATE:
pineapple wedges
spirals of lime rind

Moisten rim of a wine glass with lime juice and twirl in a saucer of sugar. Put cracked ice cubes into a cocktail shaker or screw-top jar.

Pour rum, gin and pineapple juice into shaker or jar. Shake to mix ingredients. Strain drink into a glass. Decorate with pineapple wedges and lime rind spirals.

Serves 1

YELLOW BIRD

3 ice cubes, cracked
1 measure white rum
⅓ measure Galliano
⅓ measure Cointreau
⅓ measure fresh lime juice

Put cracked ice cubes into a cocktail shaker or screw-top jar.

Pour white rum, Galliano and Cointreau into shaker or jar. Add lime juice. Shake to mix ingredients.

Put a little more ice into a glass. Strain cocktail into glass.

Serves 1

ICED PEACH DACQUIRI

1 ripe peach
1¼ measures white rum
¾ measure peach brandy
juice of ½ lime
1 teaspoon sugar syrup (see page 10), OR 1 teaspoon
  powdered sugar (see page 10)
TO DECORATE:
twist of lime rind
1 cocktail cherry

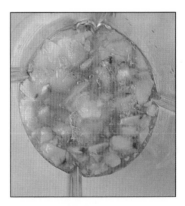

Cut a cross in skin at rounded end of peach. Place in a bowl with boiling water; after 20 seconds or so skin should easily peel off. Cut peach in half and chop flesh into a blender.

Add ice, rum, peach brandy, lime juice and sugar syrup to a blender. Mix ingredients at high speed for about 30 seconds until mixture is slushy. Pour, unstrained, into a tall glass. Decorate with a twist of lime rind and a cocktail cherry. Serve with drinking straws.

Serves 1

PARADISO

4 ice cubes, cracked
1½ measures white rum
¼ measure apricot brandy
¼ measure orange liqueur
TO DECORATE:
apricot slice
twist of lemon
twist of orange

Put half the ice into a cocktail shaker or screw-top jar. Pour rum, apricot brandy and orange liqueur into shaker or jar. Shake to mix.

Put remaining ice into a glass. Strain into glass. Decorate with an apricot slice and slices of lemon and orange twisted together.

Serves 1

MARUMBA

3 ice cubes, cracked
¾ measure dark rum
¾ measure Mandarin Napoleon liqueur
juice of ½ lemon
TO DECORATE:
long strip of mandarin rind
mandarin segments

Put ice cubes into a cocktail shaker or
screw-top jar. Pour rum and Mandarin
Napoleon into shaker or jar. Add lemon
juice.

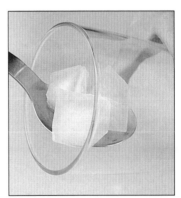

Shake to mix. Strain drink into a glass.
Decorate with mandarin rind and segments.

Serves 1

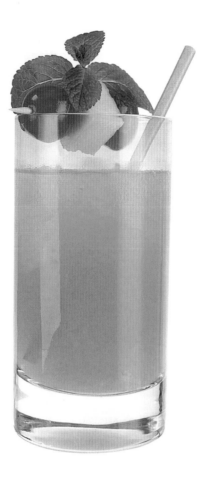

ZOMBIE

3 ice cubes, cracked
1 measure dark rum
1 measure white rum
½ measure apricot brandy
2 measures unsweetened pineapple juice
1 tablespoon fresh lime juice
2 teaspoons powdered sugar (see page 10)
TO DECORATE:
sprig of mint
maraschino cherries
fresh pineapple cubes
powdered sugar (see page 10)

Put a tall glass in the freezer to frost the outside.

Put the ice cubes into a cocktail shaker or screw-top jar. Pour the rums, apricot brandy, pineapple juice and lime juice into shaker or jar. Add sugar. Shake to mix ingredients.
Pour unstrained drink into frosted glass. Thread mint, maraschino cherries and pineapple cubes on to a cocktail stick (wooden toothpick) and place across glass. Sprinkle powdered sugar on to drink. Serve with straws.

Serves 1

WATERLOO

5 ice cubes, cracked
¾ measure white rum
¾ measure Mandarin Naploeon liqueur
1½ measures fresh orange juice
soda water, for topping up
TO DECORATE:
lightly beaten egg white
superfine sugar
half slice of orange

Frost rim of a goblet (see page 11). Put half the ice cubes into a cocktail shaker or screw-top jar. Pour rum and liqueur into shaker or jar. Add orange juice and shake.

Strain drink into goblet. Top up with soda water and decorate with orange slice. Serve with a straw.

Serves 1

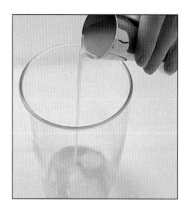

— MAI TAI —

4 ice cubes, cracked
1 measure white rum
½ measure fresh orange juice
½ measure fresh lime juice
TO DECORATE:
lightly beaten egg white
superfine sugar
fresh pineapple cubes
maraschino cherries
orange slices

Frost rim of a glass with egg white and sugar (see page 11). Put most of ice into a cocktail shaker or screw-top jar.

Pour white rum into shaker or jar. Add orange juice and lime juice. Shake to mix ingredients. Put remaining ice into a glass. Strain cocktail into glass. Decorate with pineapple cubes, maraschino cherries and orange slices.

Serves 1

— EL DORADO —

strip of orange rind
unsweetened shredded coconut
3 ice cubes, cracked
1 measure white rum
1 measure crème de cacao
1 measure advocaat
1 teaspoon grated fresh coconut OR ½ teaspoon
   unsweetened shredded coconut
TO DECORATE:
orange slices

Wipe orange rind around rim of glass, then
dip rim in unsweetened shredded coconut.
Put ice cubes into a cocktail shaker or
screw-top jar.

Pour rum, crème de cacao, advocaat and
fresh or unsweetened shredded coconut into
shaker or jar. Shake to mix ingredients.
Strain cocktail into the cocktail glass.
Decorate with orange slices. Serve with
straws.

Serves 1

SERENADE

6 ice cubes, crushed
1 measure white rum
½ measure Amaretto di Saronno
½ measure coconut cream
2 measures unsweetened pineapple juice
pineapple slices, to decorate

Put half the ice cubes into a cocktail shaker
or screw-top jar. Pour rum, Amaretto and
coconut cream into shaker or jar. Add
pineapple juice. Shake to mix ingredients.

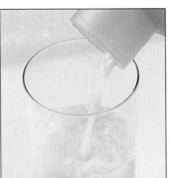

Put remaining ice into a tall glass. Strain
cocktail into glass. Decorate with pineapple
slices divided into quarters and serve with
straws.

Serves 1

GAY GALLIANO

4-5 ice cubes, cracked
1 measure rum, preferably golden
½ measure Galliano
2½ teaspoons fresh lemon juice
spiral of lemon rind, to decorate

Put ice cubes into a blender. Pour rum
and Galliano into shaker or jar. Add 2
teaspoons lemon juice. Remaining ½
teaspoon of lemon juice may be added to
taste. Mix until thick and semi-frozen.

Pour drink into a tall glass. Decorate with a
spiral of lemon rind.

Serves 1

— BLUE MOUNTAIN COCKTAIL —

ice cubes, cracked
1½ measures white rum
½ measure vodka
¼ measure Tia Maria
2 tablespoons fresh orange juice
2 teaspoons fresh lemon juice
2 teaspoons grenadine
TO DECORATE:
maraschino cherry
orange slice

Put ice into a cocktail shaker or screw-top jar. Pour rum, vodka and Tia Maria into shaker or jar. Add orange juice, lemon juice and grenadine. Shake drink to mix.

Strain into glass. Decorate with a maraschino cherry and a twisted orange slice.

Serves 1

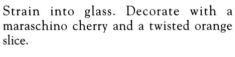

ISLAND DREAM

crushed ice
1 measure white rum
1 measure Cointreau
3½ tablespoons orange juice
2 teaspoons fresh lemon juice
1 teaspoon grenadine
TO DECORATE:
½ lemon slice
½ orange slice
maraschino cherries

Fill a small tumbler with crushed ice. Pour rum, Cointreau, orange juice, lemon juice and grenadine over ice. Stir well.

Decorate glass with ½ lemon slice, ½ orange slice and maraschino cherries. Serve with a drinking straw.

Serves 1

BOMBAY SMASH

ice cubes, cracked
4-6 sprigs of mint
1 tablespoon superfine sugar
1 measure dark rum
strip of lemon peel
orange slice, to decorate

Put mint and sugar into a medium glass.
Crush together to extract mint flavor.

Add rum and ice cubes. Stir together.
Squeeze lemon peel over top and decorate
with orange slice.

Serves 1

SCORPION

5 ice cubes, crushed
1 measure brandy
½ measure white rum
½ measure dark rum
2 measures fresh orange juice
2 teaspoons Amaretto di Saronno
2-3 dashes Angostura bitters
TO DECORATE:
½ slice orange
½ slice lemon
twist of orange rind
twist of lemon rind

Put half the ice into a cocktail shaker or screw-top jar.

Pour brandy, rums, orange juice, Amaretto and bitters into shaker or jar. Shake to mix. Put remaining ice into a goblet. Strain in cocktail. Decorate with orange and lemon slices and rinds.

Serves 1

CHAMPAGNE COCKTAIL

1 sugar cube
3 dashes Angostura bitters
½ measure cognac
Champagne, chilled, for topping up

Put sugar cube into a Champagne flute.

Sprinkle Angostura bitters on to sugar cube. Pour in cognac. Top up drink with Champagne and stir gently.

Serves 1

MELON SPRITZER

1 ripe Galia melon, about 4 lb
grated rind and juice of 1 lemon
grated rind and juice of 2 limes
1 bottle sparkling dry wine
superfine sugar, to taste
mint sprigs, to decorate

Cut melon in half and scoop out and discard
seeds. Put melon flesh in a blender with
lemon and lime rinds and juice. Blend until
smooth. Pour through a sieve, if liked.
Sweeten to taste. Chill.

To serve, half-fill cold glasses with melon
purée. Top up with sparkling wine. Decorate
with mint sprigs.

Serves 6-8

POINSETTIA

1 tablespoon Grand Marnier or Cointreau
1 measure cranberry juice
Champagne or other dry sparkling wine, chilled, for
   topping up

In a Champagne flute, or tall, slim glass,
mix liqueur and cranberry juice.

Pour in Champagne or sparkling wine.

Serves 1

MARGARITA

1 lime, halved
1 tablespoon salt
4 ice cubes, crushed
½ cup tequila
2 tablespoons orange liqueur
lime slices, to decorate

Rub rims of 2 cocktail glasses with cut lime halves. Dip rims in salt. Squeeze juice from limes into cocktail shaker or screw-top jar. Add crushed ice, tequila and orange liqueur. Shake together.

Strain drink into glasses. Decorate glasses with lime slices.

Serves 2

TEQUILA SUNRISE

3 ice cubes, cracked
4 fl oz tequila
2 tablespoons unsweetened orange or pineapple juice
1 egg white (see page 11)
2 tablespoons grenadine

Put cracked ice cubes into a cocktail shaker or screw-top jar. Add tequila, orange or pineapple juice and egg white to cocktail shaker or jar. Shake to mix ingredients.

Pour into cocktail glasses. Tilting each glass in turn, spoon in grenadine.

Serves 2

———— COLORADO ————

2-3 ice cubes, cracked
1 measure kirsch
1 measure cherry brandy
2 tablespoons heavy cream
a pair of fresh dark cherries or a maraschino cherry,
  to decorate

Put ice cubes into cockail shaker or
screw-top jar. Pour kirsch and cherry brandy
into shaker or jar. Add cream.

Shake drink to mix. Strain cocktail into a
glass. Decorate with fresh dark cherries, or a
maraschino cherry.

Serves 1

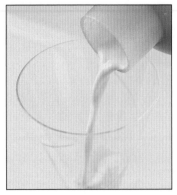

——— NELL GWYNN ———

2 ice cubes, cracked
1 measure apricot brandy
fresh orange juice
3-4 dashes orange bitters

Put cracked ice into a glass.

Pour apricot brandy over ice. Top up with orange juice. Add bitters to taste and stir.

Serves 1

SOUTHERN STAR

2-3 ice cubes, cracked
2 measures bianco vermouth
1 measure Southern Comfort

Put ice cubes into a cocktail shaker or screw-top jar. Pour vermouth and Southern Comfort into shaker or jar. Shake to mix ingredients.

Strain drink into a cocktail glass.

Serves 1

SASSY

4 ice cubes, cracked
½ measure Drambuie
2 tablespoons fresh orange juice
2 tablespoons fresh lemon juice
tonic water, for topping up
TO DECORATE:
orange slices
lemon slices

Put half of ice into a mixing glass. Pour Drambuie, orange juice and lemon juice into mixing glass. Stir together.

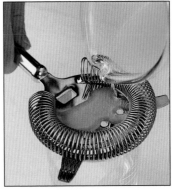

Put remaining ice into a glass. Strain cocktail into glass. Top up with tonic water. Decorate with orange and lemon slices twisted together.

Serves 1

FOXY LADY

3 ice cubes, cracked
1 measure Amaretto di Saronno
½ measure crème de cacao
1 measure heavy cream
TO DECORATE:
lightly beaten egg white
finely grated or chopped dark chocolate, or cocoa
   powder mixed with a little superfine sugar
chocolate dragee

Frost rim of a cocktail glass with egg white and dark chocolate, or cocoa mixed with superfine sugar (see page 11).

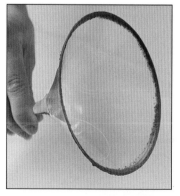

Put ice into a cocktail shaker or screw-top jar. Pour Amaretto and crème de cacao into shaker or jar. Add cream. Shake to mix drink. Strain into glass. Top with dragee or finely grated or chopped chocolate.

Serves 1

VELVET GLOVE

4 ice cubes, cracked
1 measure Tia Maria or Kahlua
½ measure Amaretto di Saronno
1 measure heavy cream
TO DECORATE:
lightly beaten egg white
ground coffee or powdered instant coffee
finely grated or chopped chocolate (optional)

Frost rim of a small brandy balloon glass with egg white and ground coffee beans or powdered instant coffee (see page 11). Put half the ice into a cocktail shaker or screw-top jar. Put remaining ice into glass.

Pour Tia Maria or Kahlua and Amaretto into shaker or jar. Add cream. Shake to mix drink and strain into glass. Top with ground coffee, or finely grated or chopped chocolate.

Serves 1

PASSIONFRUIT COOLER

thinly pared rind of 1 lemon
2 teaspoons sugar
6 ripe passionfruit
1 large, very ripe mango, peeled and chopped
juice of 1 lemon
juice of 1 lime
ice cubes, to serve
soda water, chilled, for topping up
lemon and lime slices, for decoration

Put lemon rind in a stainless steel saucepan with ⅔ cup water. Bring to the boil, stirring to dissolve sugar. Boil for 1 minute. Remove from heat, cover and cool.

Refrigerate until very cold. Scoop seeds from passionfruit into a nylon sieve and rub firmly with the back of a spoon to remove all the flesh. Discard seeds. Purée mango flesh and mix with passionfruit flesh. Strain in lemon and lime juices. Put ice cubes into 4 tall glasses. Add passionfruit mixture and top up with soda water. Decorate with lemon and lime slices. Serve at once with straws.

Serves 4

— PINEAPPLE & MANGO PUNCH —

1 ripe pineapple
½ large, ripe mango, peeled and chopped
⅔ cup traditional ginger beer
sparkling mineral water, for topping up
lemon or lime juice, to taste

Using a large, sharp knife, slice top off pineapple. Scoop fruit from center without piercing shell. Reserve shell. Discard tough core. About ½lb of the flesh and juice should remain.

Put pineapple flesh and juice, mango and ginger beer into a blender. Mix until smooth. Dilute to drinking consistency with sparkling mineral water. Flavor drink with lemon or lime juice to taste. Pour into reserved pineapple shell. Serve with straws.

Serves 2

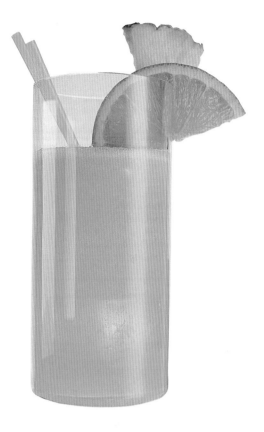

— ORANGE & PINEAPPLE CRUSH —

1 pineapple, about 2 lb
1¼ cups fresh orange juice
2 tablespoons fresh lemon juice
12 ice cubes
soda water or sparkling mineral water, for topping up
orange slices and pineapple chunks to decorate

Slice across pineapple. Cut off skin. Remove core and 'eyes' and chop flesh. Put into blender or food processor. Add orange juice and blend for 1-2 minutes. Strain through nylon sieve into a jug and press firmly with the back of a spoon to extract all the juice. Strain in lemon juice and stir.

Put 3 ice cubes into each of 4 tall glasses. Divide fruit juices among glasses. Top up with soda water or sparkling mineral water. Decorate glasses with orange slices and pineapple chunks. Serve with straws.

Serves 4

INDEX